HAECCEITIES

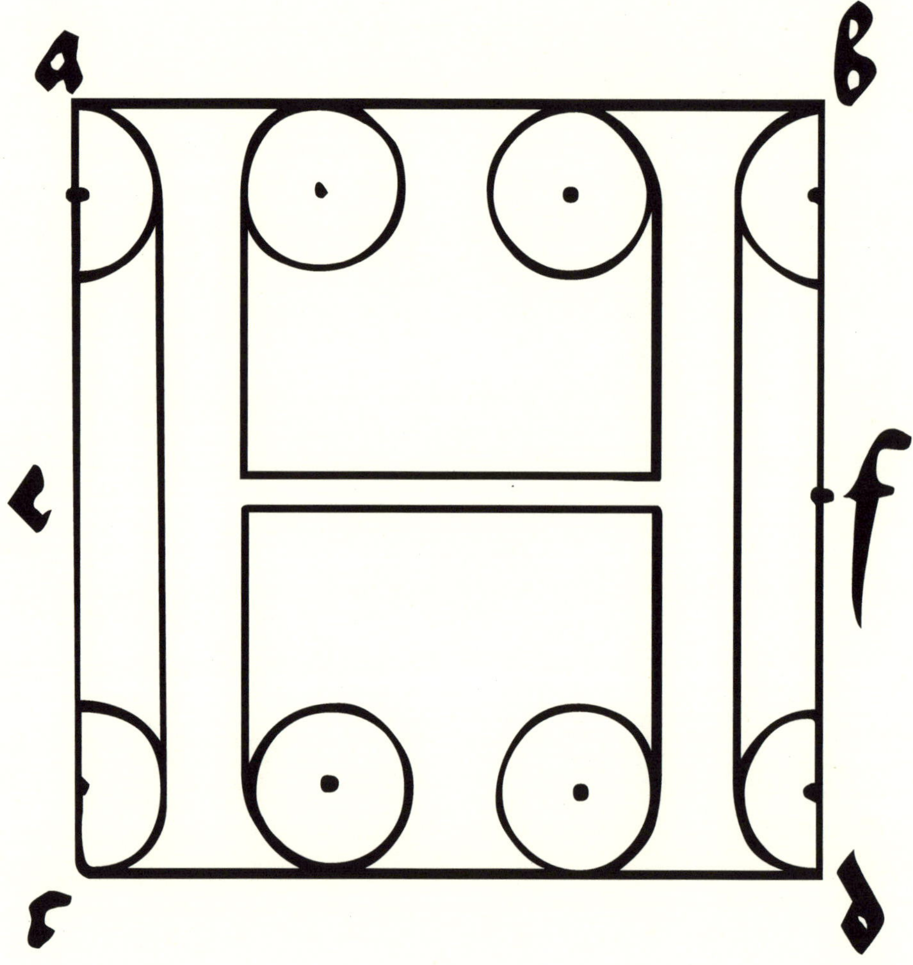

a
b
c
d
e
f

HAECCEITIES
MICHAEL CROSS

CUNEIFORM PRESS / 2010

LCCN: 2010929840
ISBN: 978-1234567897

Distributed by:
Small Press Distribution
1341 Seventh Street
Berkeley, CA 94710-1403
510-524-1668 or toll-free
800-869-7553
www.spdbooks.org

Address all editorial inquiries to:
Cuneiform Press
University of Houston-Victoria
School of Arts and Sciences
Victoria, TX 77901

∞

The paper on which this book is printed meets the minimum requirements of
American National Standard for Information Sciences – Permanence of Paper for
Printed Library Materials, ANSI Z39.48–1984

This book was made possible, in part, through the generous support from the School
of Arts and Sciences, University of Houston-Victoria and friends of Cuneiform Press.

ACKNOWLEDGMENTS

My thanks to the editors of the following publications, who saw fit to print many of these poems as they slowly materialized over the years: *a little gentle seen, Buffalo Vortex, Double Room, Gam, little red leaves, P-Queue, Try!,* and *War and Peace.*

"Cede" and "Throne" originally appeared as chapbooks thanks to the efforts of the Vigilance Society and Dos Press respectively.

And to the following, who significantly contributed to this manuscript (in one way or another) as it was drafted: Taylor Brady, Thom Donovan, Eli Drabman, Zack Finch, Katja Geldhof, Rob Halpern, Myung Mi Kim, C.J. Martin, Rich Owens, Andrew Rippeon, Leslie Scalapino, Kyle Schlesinger, and Krzyzstof Ziarek.

"The Pales" is for Myung Mi Kim
"Cardinal" is for Eli Drabman and Krzysztof Ziarek
"Sacred" is for Thom Donovan and C.J. Martin
"Pax" is for Carl Andre

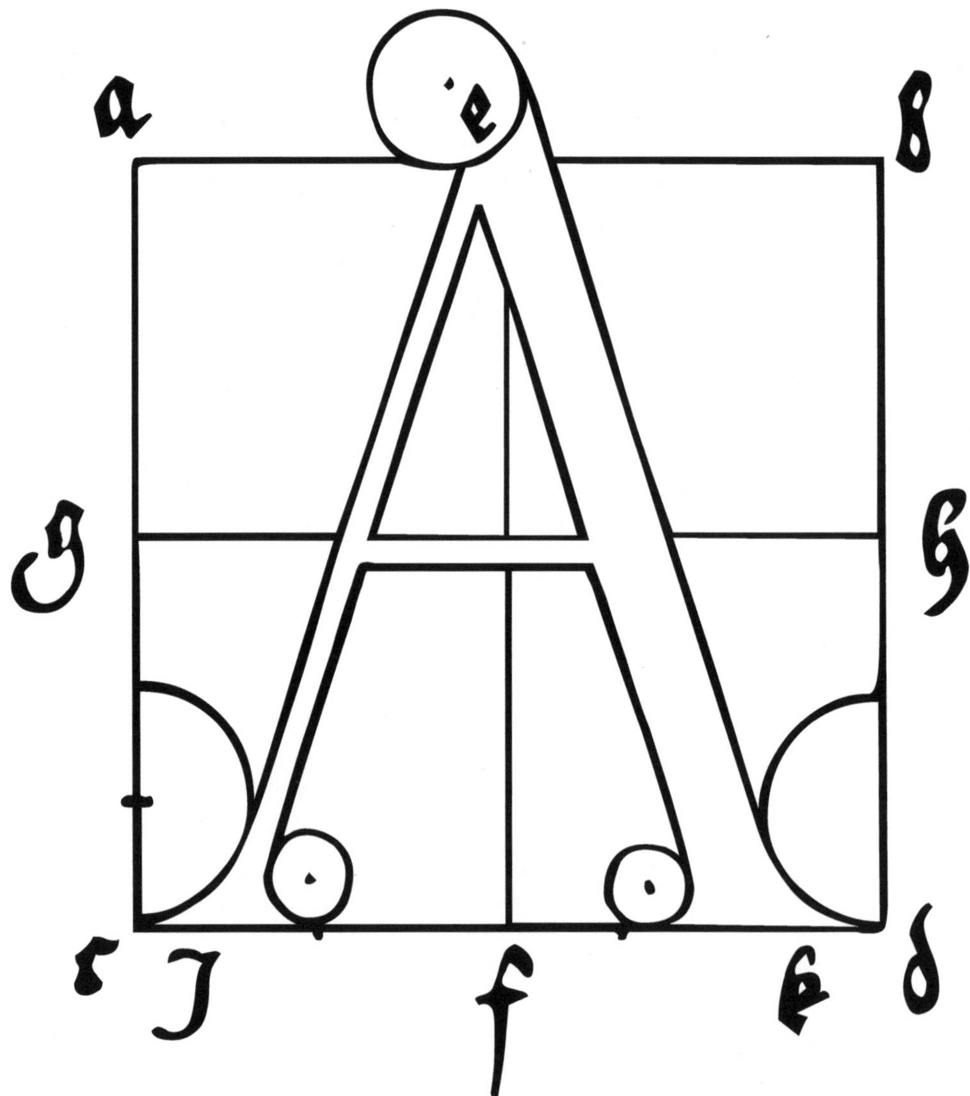

After he had been born in the postoffice he began to practice his
mouth with a new language. He could not imagine persons to
listen to the new language. He had not invented politics.
— Jack Spicer

I would say a thing is a hole in a thing it is not.
— Carl Andre

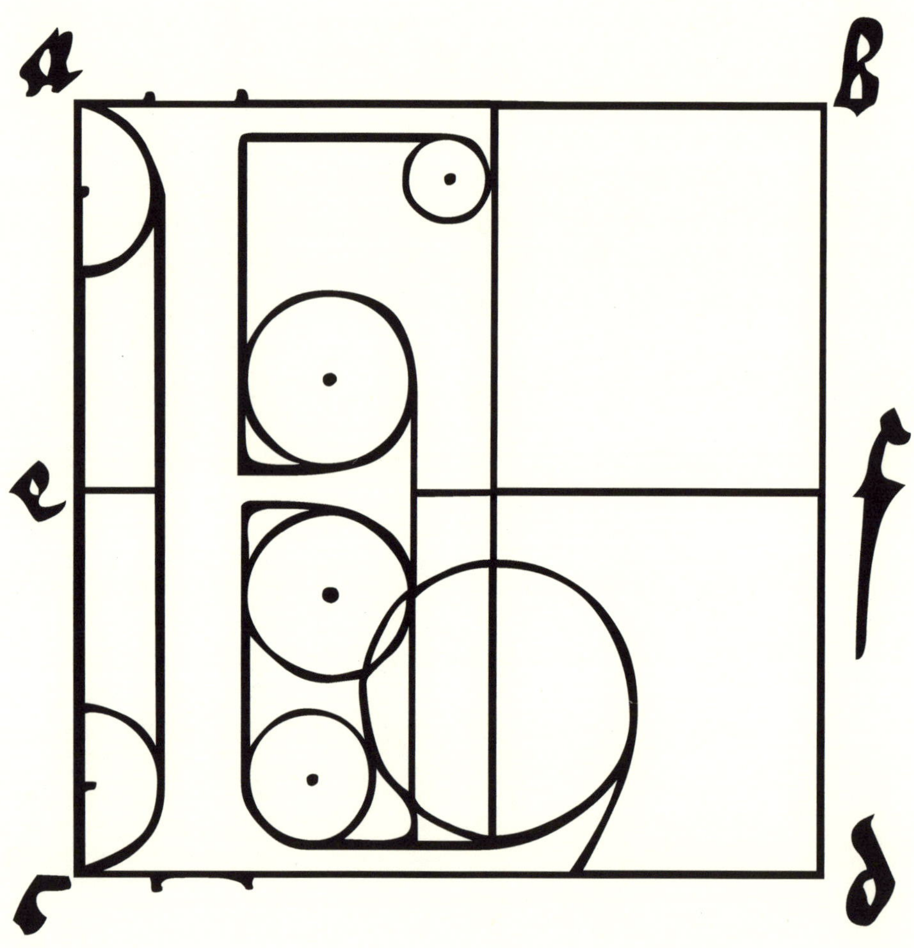

a
B
e
f
c
d

CONTENTS

The Pales   11

Plinth Course   23

Cardinal   35

Cede   43

Sacred   57

Throne   69

Pax   83

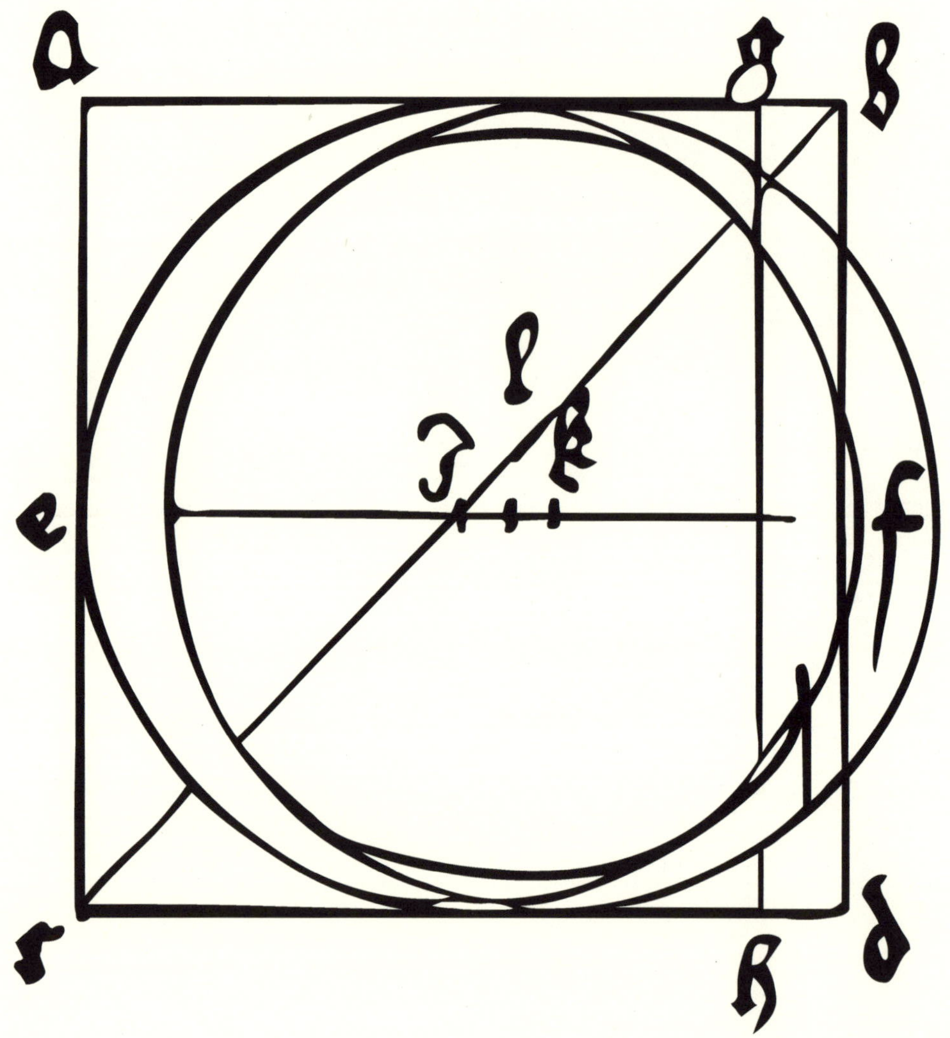

THE
PALES

It is as labor, and not as communication, that the
subject in art comes into its own.
— Theodor Adorno

The possibility of producing, of fecundating the fields and the
herds is given to rite whose least servile operative forms are
aimed, through a concession, at cutting the loses from
the dreadful violence of the divine world.
— Georges Bataille

Thy fields, propitious Pales, I rehearse;
And sing thy pastures in no vulgar verse
— Virgil

•

alacrity at time and yet the hulkish ness

silt licks modality means better ness there

belied how marshal made hon

there catch and mannered tone

•

in so awake to fell, to be fallen

augury creatures of hotly purse

augury in eyes such and in such wise

once the cheek noth tongue

sounds the very manner of handing

holds the hoarsome say

ice pack the cut

•

a hand on the air came

calm traffic way the air came

calm sleeved sez conduce the men

hold eyen wept metal vat sez boss

stop the invocation say

metre is a cinch hon

•

and portent shape fetters off the slant roof

teeming made impossible hear

demotically holds synthete pales and holds

portent shape letters turnt the cant

•

longing right for some ballast

apropos, see, tethered the hulk frond

lowly tithed so very low met

prone inveterate ness meant

salve by which the city comes

•

sang oft so tautly so

stave mar might buoyant men

so work so little node the fronded husk

drones daylobe, terribly has one

charge only, one drome

•

the many hundred wing-lit hives

so saucily so the onerous fever kenning

the coupling come coupling bound by night

this little things strung plenty like

yield the hollow soft hem the light

•

thus the waste mate skies

bodely some mindful rung

the meter, my sadly,

perimeters leafsome

as if sulking eyes

a further place to hunt

•

as lithe might cut the

lushery the mooded

swallows the whole cherry bloom

the mighty pyre further

there green the pyre further

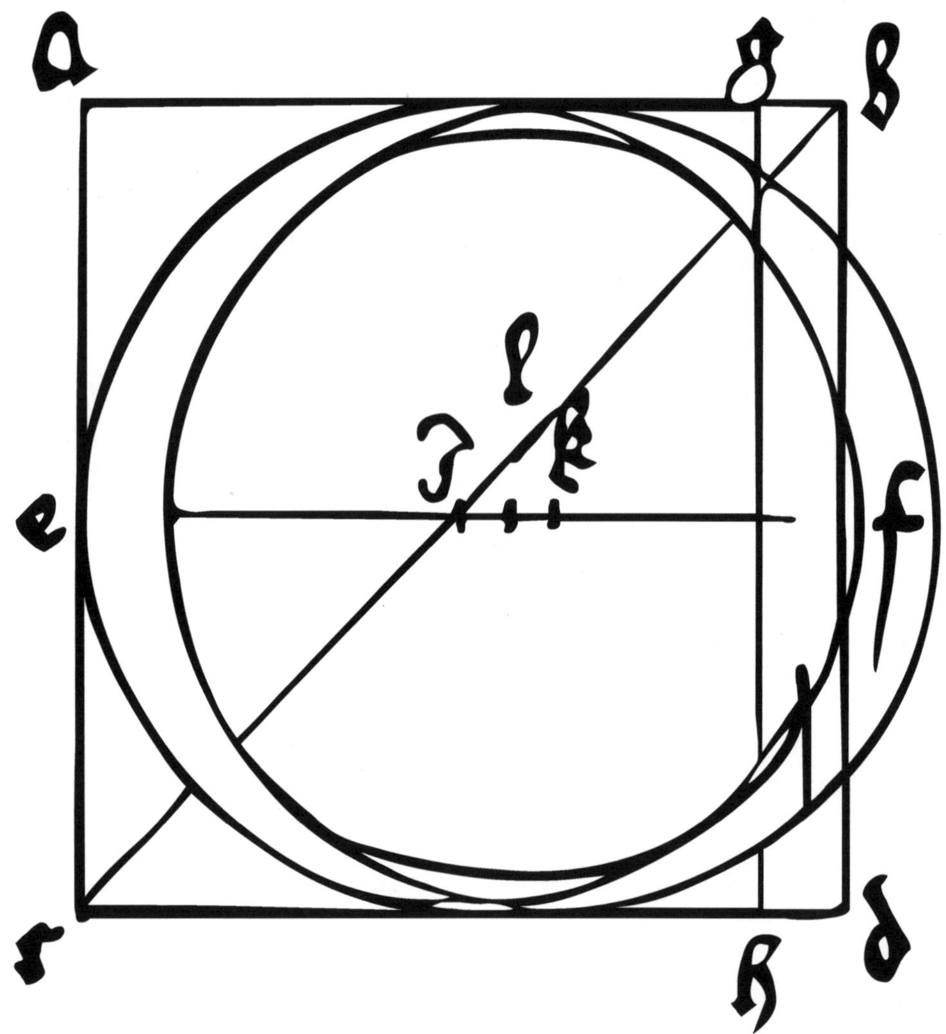

PLINTH
COURSE

A colossus, rather, a certain kolossos which erects itself as measure.
["S'érige en mesure": also, "rises up in time"
(in the musical sense of "in time").
— Jacques Derrida

...parallels and affinities here are not operations toward a
philosophy but operations of a fabrication,
open possibilities of design.
— Robert Duncan

The strife that is brought into the rift and thus set back
into the earth and thus fixed in place is the figure...
Figure is the structure in whose shape the rift
composes itself. This composed rift is
the fugue of truth's shining.
— Martin Heidegger

ontically before the sea quoth a large cobalt bench

soldered breast-width fans a great wing's

taciturn, yellow on the willow plank, ventricle

and plenum, the numb parchment of boxwraithes

sore by sole crest [singly] suited to the tarpaulin

row set the crop set swatch

Sweaters of the corpuscle, twain labor the lynx

heads adazzle the outer compound of the pastor-kind, a plan fabric,

capricious even by name as vulnerable gratis reckoning

the armature of the beloved—*braces! this gale discriminates those*

handsome working—the Vain Command becoming liquor, cormorants at matins, truants from the balustrade confide shirtless

grandling the sky in threes, the subject [from the balcony] calls:

gesticulations near you, or, *culture-wash the cormorant*

in other words, the balcony concedes it's calumny

it says, the swallow turns, this is the tertial, the guerdon, the distaff afterimage's as little evidence as turn

carapace, the green-plan's tertiary

at once drawn its plumed top-mast

brick green awash the southern lip of the pelages

ghostlier, pathic, the revenant fecund, at once

the sylph pour porcelain from the ears

of thousand dead, the porcelain from the head

of Entellus, wrists bound with the hide gauntlets

of Eryx, Alcides, fuller blood in youth, the threshold

the vast bulk upborne by Dares in torpid age

Porcelain strewn her snows at either face her word

cirrus vine the lattice

rather, first vine, *Minor Wood*,

the orioles are five in the trees, long to pass

equivalence for *taxon*, rather, first troubles

arbiters of wood, saddling caprice, the wooded;

sublimny says *wood*, liminal, *the nave walk dear away*

they say *swallow* somatically the crow against the face

against the greater weight of face, jocund, teem-eyed, oxen

louche figure on the floor

tends crinoline, felt catch around the fall

PAINT ROSE, PAINT ROSE along the atelier in milk

I, *purloin*, the louche, *maudlin the day song*

detritus anyway as the switch is sweat

not brass and tumid in the heat of the animal milk—

garishly mint, onericish, strange to wake *with* mint,

into mint—louche pace the fall, hardly yield a trap

its costumed, geometrically impossible hands

what whitens a paucity of white

felicities of brick color, the color

blue-eared by which such leaps

align themselves to whetting

the second white of the socius

the light coloring of the man with the butterfly body

on the one hand, where it shades the white total against

the mint alluvium like a fingerprint of white

efficacy of tar and straw

dulcet morass, Maladroit wrought buttressed

by the half-mooring peristyle—*prurient first-drawn*

nude drawn *nude* in blood on the grey tarp

say gestic machinations of their somber

wit writ large, writ small and large again

in that Vitalism by virtue of the Sylphic Aire to wit

the canticle reanimates *descant, descant* the tenor, blithe, agog twilight's once piebald cum twilight

once paint-eyed prey made bramble shape

gable from gable, vermeiled mammal-white,

whitest white both heel both ankle like

thigh-glass shapes at once brass, once figured, there chalk figures

I, *pleasure*, pleasure the brittle taxon map shadowed

shape to swallow—pleaser's silk cantle traps

the face, paucus webs these eyes place *this* here,

this, the face I please, sisal detexted a surface

from vermillion, the demesne one angle

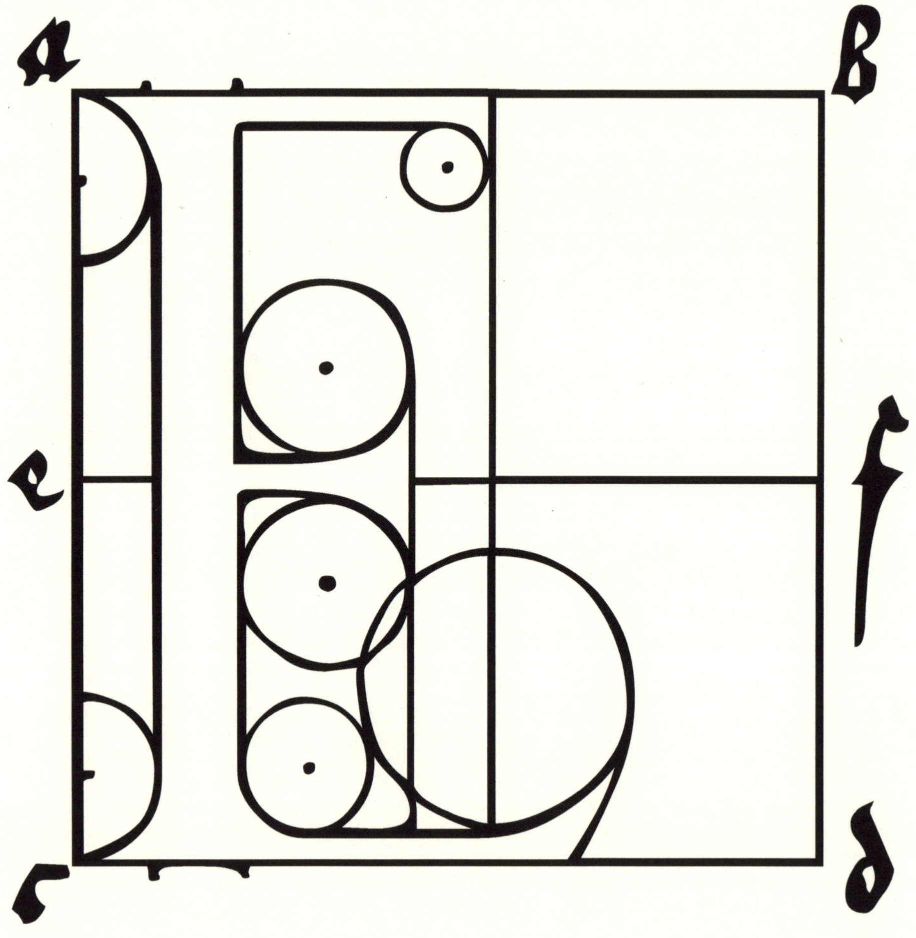

this is the orange measurement of the lines
as I design them.
— Robert Duncan

What seems clear is, that two dimensions as suface for plastic
attack is once more prime. And with all perspective as aid
gone, the whole Renaissance. Even line gone.
And maybe color—as too easy.
— Charles Olson

certain of the eyes have loose

the girl balloons pumiced-soft agleam for too

phatically red in the red grass phatically trine

lodged in the tree's three and limpid branch

thread aroint pressures kids against

the crane skree the tree's least holden

cup balloon, halidom and purse

ten-slender since the plume imbues the feathered

but bespoken plume, fanned-feathers shuff ten

ten grate marble fosse avec a single-banded kid

environ for an opening WORLD

reminds kid the stun slit by which, plummeting in-ness

bulbs strung, made strident by the copper

hood of *boredom*, an engagement

with which plummets poverty of WORLD

foaming stunts, the feathered back retreats depravity as such blackweed and waxen mint as horizontally sward boys

alabasterly bred bright breaking ornithology's in the corner

by falls, a single rail facing tongues

holds an open fold of orange rings

mitts the tray, pushing off a history I face toward

the figure for time imbues figures

florid spangled-shape kids, a swollen sharp Inhibitor

enough to cede the errer

at least its orange band shuttling EARTH

pulpous, contrast of the violent tangerine against the white

the rain plait, threads the waist still slake

elsewise, responding to the taper of the wolves

they fallow, moist and leggéd dure their brilliant shapes

the tumid molt of light in three partition black

gloaming: *presentation, darstellung,* the meadow in the throat

of red-vinyl wolves licking the Open's wound as it withdrawals

the stilling of its image: in 1938, the turning does

to thinking for a turn involve

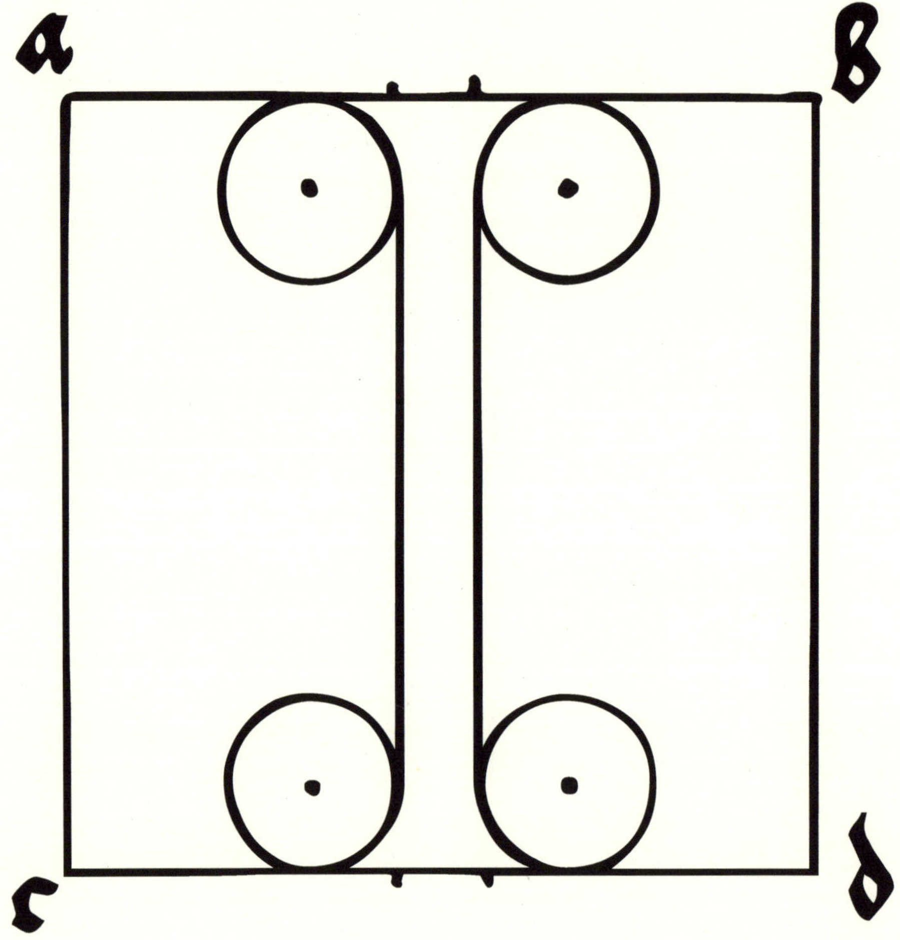

CEDE

Every animal is in the world like water in water...
— Georges Bataille

Because the gush of color is held back, it mobilizes
more violence, potentializes the double energy:
first the full encircling ring, the black line,
incisive, definitive, then the flood
of broad chromatic scales
in a wash of color.
— Jacques Derrida

The man who is "absorbed" by the object that he is
contemplating can be "brought back to himself"
only by a Desire; by the desire to eat,
for example.
— Alexandre Kojève

We cannot say concerning a wolf which eats another wolf that
it violates the law decreeing that ordinarily *wolves do not
eat one another*. It does not violate this law; it has
simply found itself in circumstances where
the law no longer applies.
— Georges Bataille

have oaths evinced the metron still and still each sovereign rest despite the socius

and the white they race toward; the total of the social white takes honey as to face the abdomen

in excess of a tangerine encampment, such that haecceities neither fold themselves free the lapping

ancillary mass at the ankles of the ring's arrangement by which behavior makes itself a lenity wares laden partially with silhouette enmasse, the lime trees

the sacer green impugn to cast the Hegemon both teeth and brook

the Cardinal and its epigone on foot to face, turn and face the Hegemon

face the fissure of the sacer on one, EARTH, its nexus of tags by which WORLD,

surface of embattlement, the other (crimson) lyric-less Despiser were one to say the gnosis once lye from fallow bits to tire, staged by the *doxa* of the police

folkways want me tarred aside the rood a stealer short partition and surrection

animal has thrice the cusp, mauled me by its lawlessness in so far as *demos,*

the supplement stage a single fissure by right alembic tongue

mouth's variety of black shape to condition the surface of the ring for the figure

of the wolf and fawn; how the king's two bodies still a center of consensus,

the grackle paws the concrete as it flees

lynch and gyre squared by hand and level at the lip of law

there by horse pins rivet to the canticle wants barren there

needs the sure hand squares the hunter by its meats

it weighs there for to leave the copse, tarry by the slack pile, law says

Logik—draws on owl to disengage the chalk springs lit upon entrance

nothing more: master from entelechy, a hide enthinned

dead heat and center shore the signet bell, wind ascribes its noumenon

pronounce the trapper's mount the eyelet's teeth and limb

the other wants its fatigable lip submerged, the bottle lip, swoll lymph

by prime leges couched leged and garbed by strake of nerves

its lot endures the king's synchronal thrones at either end his word but one quint the coruscent figure, disport plumes and fife

as drops arranged the surface of the strake planks

once more, the gestalt two, each to each a boon of catholic sympathies

to reach or leap away the Disinhibitor by way of drone, dram, *doxa*

lex records the quietus of Spirit, cylindrical drums ground to rapport

flattened flush a sixth

cadence and the will affined each trope to sight and sight to see in keys

the time of which apportioned share, matter and its relumine command

its word then the sepulchral, buckram, gauche, affixed by carbon tress

draped slipshod from the scepter to the scythe

nomos finally holden to a kind of cribbed proximity

tensor by the throat, it says the plover there, matrices of animal and hand

whiteness can one add to white but white course proffer at the skirt of cause

it was Twombly and wholly in some other reference to how a lake we know in common

yields the business of a mark by four pendulant inflections

a boxy vent as to air the swan its ebullient row of grace no more

nothing of the shaled discs, unfettered ware's ledgers of the rout, volumes of

yet dregs deterred in throes of vulgar matting so a sense serves mercy: *umwelt*

by its compass, proffered frame by which each prey to each each mouth to each to hand bands for police, pocketed trice, light banded veiling threads the matter and its *geist*

the slate jut marks an outcropping clay, peasant boots their collars give what art reveals

by how the sovereign's hand, cloying in the mirror as the codicil by virtue of its frames

replete, restitute, dark circles on the white stay for *hills / earth / sky / night / clouds* to be rendered sans stock of crux and wont, logged above the *demos* and the stage

like Pound on Mencius on Confucius, (later) Olson on Twombly:

what whiteness can one add to white, what candor in the face of the ring of address

in Pisa say, for Twombly, the frame maintains its course of shape

the frame-abyss, Apollo in the woods, lake-red for sacrifice and use candor is enough to say the swallow at the sovran's tongue

an *aufheben* at least the trauma and to grasp—*begriff*—to grasp and fork

the cantor of his paréd throat; here the Tlingit coffin is a fosse said

scored the rest, one hundred twenty-seven times at rest the death par-ergon

candor lends its name to cede we see the matron and her switch betwixt Apollo's

four bronz'd tongues: the rest its name, rather, cede it as a legacy

Cowls, hoods and habits with thir wearers tost / Long after, now unpeopl'd, and untrod

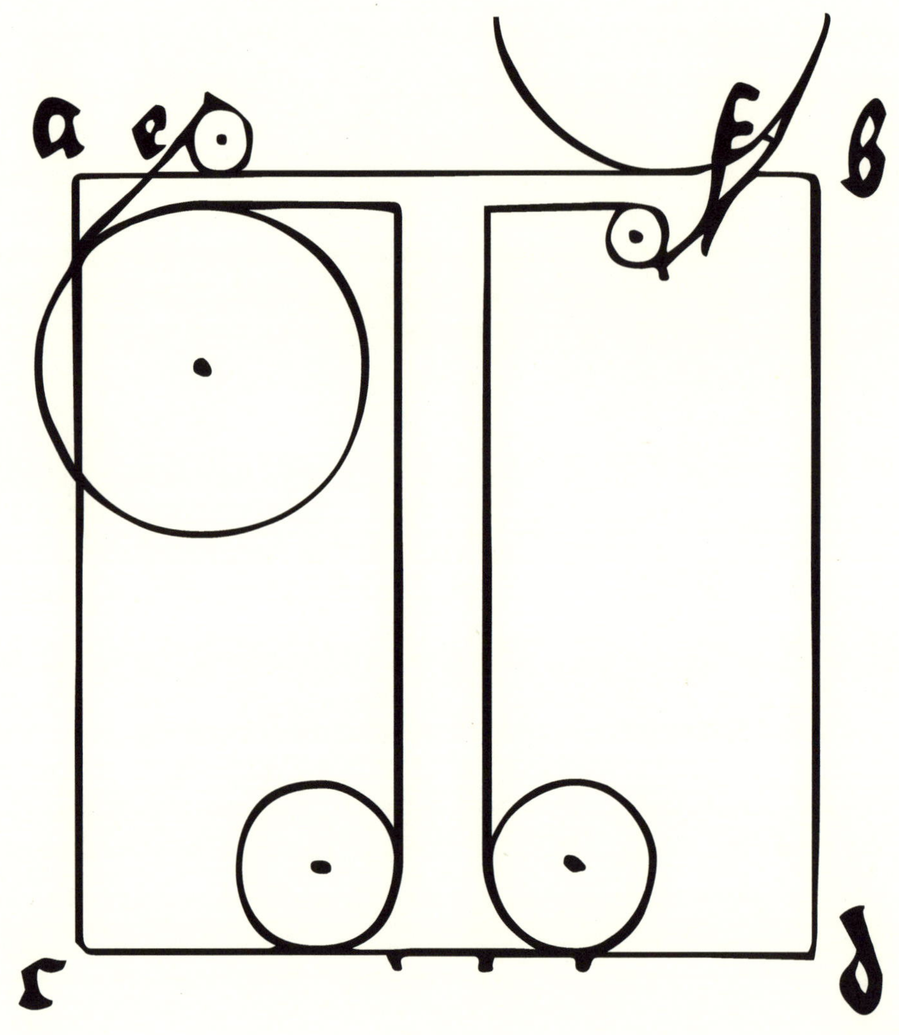

SACRED

Evental grace governs a multiplicity in excess of itself, one that is
indescribable, superabundant relative to itself as well as
with respect to the fixed distributions of the law.
— Alain Badiou

For the abyss is the poet's figure for the perpetual suspension of the
right measure or law—that crisis, that "state of exception"
in which, sent on our way by the gods, we are—
for the time being—destined to live.
— David Michael Kleinberg-Levin

What is called "grace" is the capacity of a postevental
multiplicity to exceed its own limit, a limit that has
a commandment of the law as its dead cipher.
— Alain Badiou

foregone for what's wanting the bridge sez the size of the *quodlibet*

twenty-some casts (2001, 900 x 510 x 240 cm) according to gauge accordingly resin to gauge

scant forth tuned his plinth abut the Square, in-set coat disclose

the Tangerine dais as the *count-for-one*, then, thousands of mouths in the round,

black resin LAW in each slit has an animal upright, lash against the Ister, all

whilst warrant the monarch's cairn, 'his' trestle (1765-1837) vantage for the pigeon

certainly bound by militant pitch certainly viscous amber

slag against the asphalt does to thinking for a turn involve the militant wants the pass a bare right planar face, circa 1848:

a hand at degrees against the ribs—hock or tarsus, knee or stifle, brisket, feathering

this is a grid according to length and breadth, mantled against the ribcage

opens out munitions piece—the flank I counter, munitions in pantone grays

presumably liters of blood wet the pavement, pierce Récamier, married to recline

at the chaise for François Gerard demands her bare pig's kind of lawlessness

or else the leap from *condition* to lake-red-belts adjacent the asphalt's blood

from Ashura, once intoxication of interior: machete as the rite null set two skulls slightly askant as the scale of communion and the police draped

summa (*whole*) crushed velvet, C, supremast, girder forms an intercessor for

what's inside and what leads from the shoulder of the lion

mouth full-twined mail (entwined scales) or the face in repose of one slate

here the joist immured snakes and worms cant cede in lieu of a bronzed

yoke wagging from the firth at croisillon nord: the corpses in fans

breast-width at the crest south and west enforced walls of the thirteenth

century, the bodied knots of incisors against the barricades of the fifteenth,

these veils tear the eyes this sovereign paraclete, more LOW inside, cerates both alum / portage *purely formal void* as anterior place holder,

one margin slightly landed, Sovran—repose // serried ranks,

the "Hexe" moored higher if deterred this special rank its diagrammed grounds

hundreds by the ankles of a steel pylon, in other words, the lawlessness I've swoll

the fundament's juridical torque so they won't see the liter or the mote

Peter Eisemen's *House VI* for the ENCLOSERS say a *strophe*,

from pewter's repose've wandered / from one convex strophe to a standstill

descendible: *the colonized future may be something like one of Veblan's*

"imponderables," as Zukofsky cites, and the blank becomes the only space from which

to unsettle the habit of its axiomatic power in the interest of an other future //

grace this set's imponderable tympan is to sound between relief and its impression

the recessed face of a pediment, juridical sites of dissensus because on this one,

the resin slightly elevated, it's a room, the *demos*, three elements of plastic

and urethane foam (prolix plinths)

the second plaster in relief to *Breathless*, lake-fans asymmetry,

lake-red symmetrical rivulets, alluvial fans one print in the window's

an octagon in Algeria this one octagon *Kenya Boran* (1974) removed to Houston

and finally Rice once back against the eight to view the rhombus (brown/shed/slake)

above the ziggurat and falls: grace in the light of the rhombus—*Spirit's watted filament*

in whose hands lie means, dope and cue of one's own *dure //* (chapter/verse)

ochereous and lynx-barred in lengthening might;

Patience! and you shall reach the biding place!

Here are lynxes   Here are lynxes,

Is there a sound in the forest

*   of pard or of bassarid*

or crotale   or of leaves moving

sweaters of the corpuscle, twain labor, the lynx heads dazzle red grace of sellotape and air paired next 'folk' heads sleckit, cowrin

folk for the serotype of grace seemed lately plait, agnate by a toxin

as many wolves as bird-roads, red scotch such vast, timorous interface

sans surface dimension so to socius as 'white eschatology' in Twombly's Coronation

of Seostis, his socle, frame, pedestal, an infinite sovereign efflux, fens drained, its waste

Enclosure arrived at Helpstone in 1809 to mount and did duration's chalk and charcoal

matrices held by condition of score—held to grooves and yet to flute the rim—held by

abeyance of white, chariot volant athwart the grass air held to—the chariot

harbors calm, seven frames in bed when you age a gilt wink of art's sovereignty

swoll on the general matrices aver to contact each nominal surface a face,

each press and rivet face, tocsin, period of vibration off the tangerine ring of autonomy

horn's portraits prolix matte bulbs for eyes how weather renders the dome identically vacuous, carriage on the trunk blushed orange

as a product of policing some six by ten grills a jerk from the down-orange grip

of plumule descending its neck; he's radiating, this man, somatic folds of deep ontic

orange limbic arcs —slacks sticking from the hedge mark a rim of dissensus, Scalapino's

event horizon, yellow circle-concepts sitting on the thorax reading for corpses a dozen

balloons from the vantage above the field of bodies, painting Lesage's sublime

symbolic composition of the spiritual world with tunneling lamp recurrent as the vortices

of 'Zodiac Houses': contra passione, contra mille acque, contra fonte, contra voce,

contra requiem, contra the fold's lip the deep orange pleat, its intimate orange fosse—

I draw a circle, I draw a cluster of arcs from the circle labeled *monads*,

I write WORLD and EARTH

howls like for force in claret discs, five bins a cise degrees of touch

one spine thread the socius thread ecru rings around the glass vitrine

at the center of the yard *and near my kith for that will sore me shend*

boat spikes five and ten against the wraithe's braid fall

two sheets off the ring of intelligence face the wash obliterates red points'

diaphanous film the lip of *rest* lengthwise cuz the dreams done, vertically wash

against the chink I hear the face, formally I court to count for one,

abgrund holds won't speak for normative grace a pound of flesh the subject holds

there is a difference from which to square flesh here there is a difference

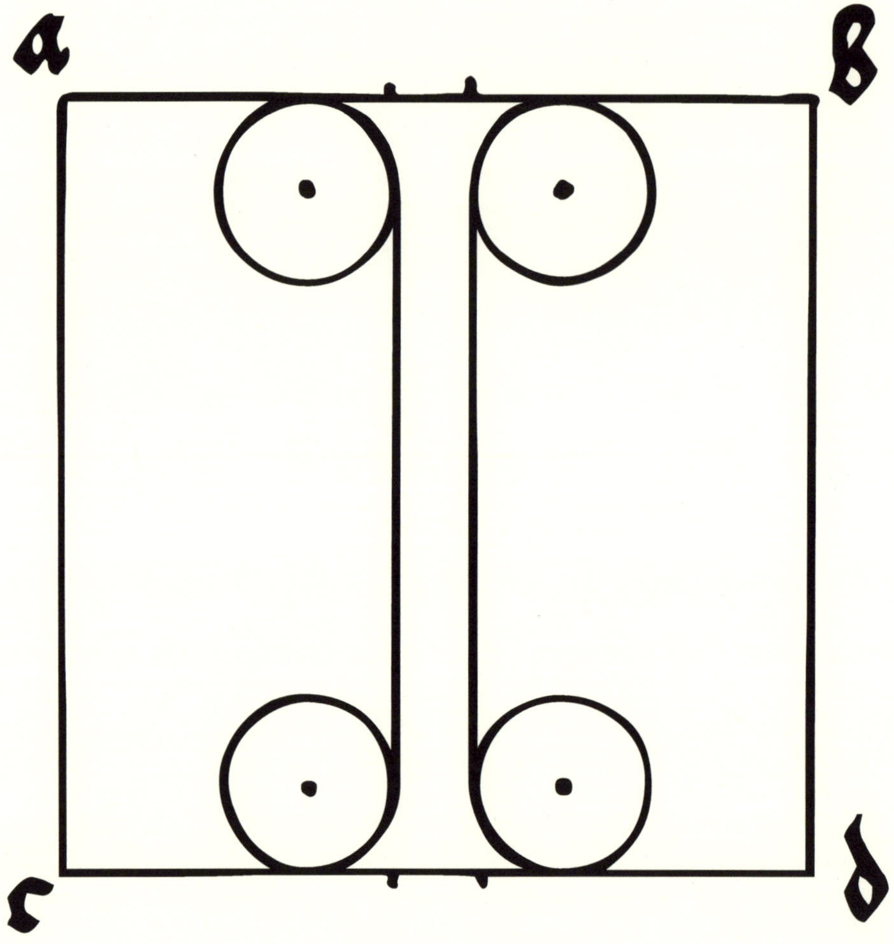

THRONE

Once you try to embrace an absolute geometric circle the
naked loss stays with you like a picture echoing.
— Jack Spicer

Will you drive me to madness only there to know me?
vomiting images into the place of the Law!
— Robert Duncan

thetic

earth halves for licit and unsanctity

as a crystal's red-gold locks

draw paren to the sun brand

as to sun I tell this guy

is water in water, bottleneck the dynast's

hand by bore flayed boxwood

lip to lave by lawmen's banded eyes

bunches in the hand the same as me

poised upon the polished fats a wedge

erst grace and sublimate, befell a gauze *bon mot*

sarx/pneuma

beside its *anomos* the christ's vulpine

sonance, sea-foam, brume

ell openly inclement

to vetting folks

I seen at the carwash

iterant's catch at the choke

for pleather thins in white

rims the place one wants a world for

sacerdotally, at least, the seam

in the hood I face

salverforms

supine in lisle hoods

how I speak for a posse

is steam purls, that that's my word

sways a bevy whom light, stag,

and motionless wedge this felted not yes

beneath the noncolor honors nothing

to not noncolor, *pistis* for love

so cleft your finger's pledge

for itself self-suffrages the horse

you hang a place on

meridian

wills toward itself in that it bans

enspathed the nowt to lunge

these throated brick cravats

by flagon's cut crystal

at the heart of the crystal

before the throne of the spadix

for literal, dowel from the mouth

hood makes a crescent mouth

its teeth, each lettered by which

for too, two-handed thrush

precutaneous

what visage does, debeller, razed, expiating

bas, our auctor wedged *da* twixt

the visor's amice grey made gaze

to palm some steely rubric-a-touch

harnessed her face lacks thingnesses sides

between the heat of the subject and the heat

of her lawfulness, sighs against the pressure, kid,

wrinkles, bellows, apophatic facing

the subject's front to come

foresting

otherwise all would will alone

against the heat, thatch for thatch

by dint save entropy's dreigh

nominal face face-flush

nominal dell sweating what quodlibet

thumbs what hydromel-ground

rents mitts, teeth in each

lobbed fist could we any

we the form in gauze curtains

no wind is the kings…

partage

before a sitter, supine, cygneous arched

operative folds the blooder's mouth

to cover to crown by cunicle cover:

incline from whence my breath,

prevenient *and* subsequent,

gives circular acanthus by thought

to smother the pleats what for more

pleats, grace begging vain fluorescence

blitz

porphyry bore a rebus that

lambent by a nacreous

glaze, mottled modular

nodes, each flayed

palm rapine and exly rackt

the *vexierbild* asks the filch

lucent by the drain's spate

of cocytus, Terrifier, eyes gleed

faced *charis* as an impasse

dehiscent that they will

aggregates where we find them

rope bridge

ell-squared bronx split

papered gold-gild planks canvassed

what wound about the trestle of the void

sites by mitigation the crozier's curve

and such shapes a plate point

by which spathe hood beveled

tight around the sockets, pinna,

coil cast, harls split from ridge

to bress to base so that what light

lops the people from the mob

nunc age

what feeds me to ashes

repine in wishes, teeth

to haul the mort above

the ice, refracts as does

the periclase gold, folds

water water, steam

and the cathedral folds

patron of the culp the

turbine's centrifugal calcified

fists, St. Pairs the seated aires

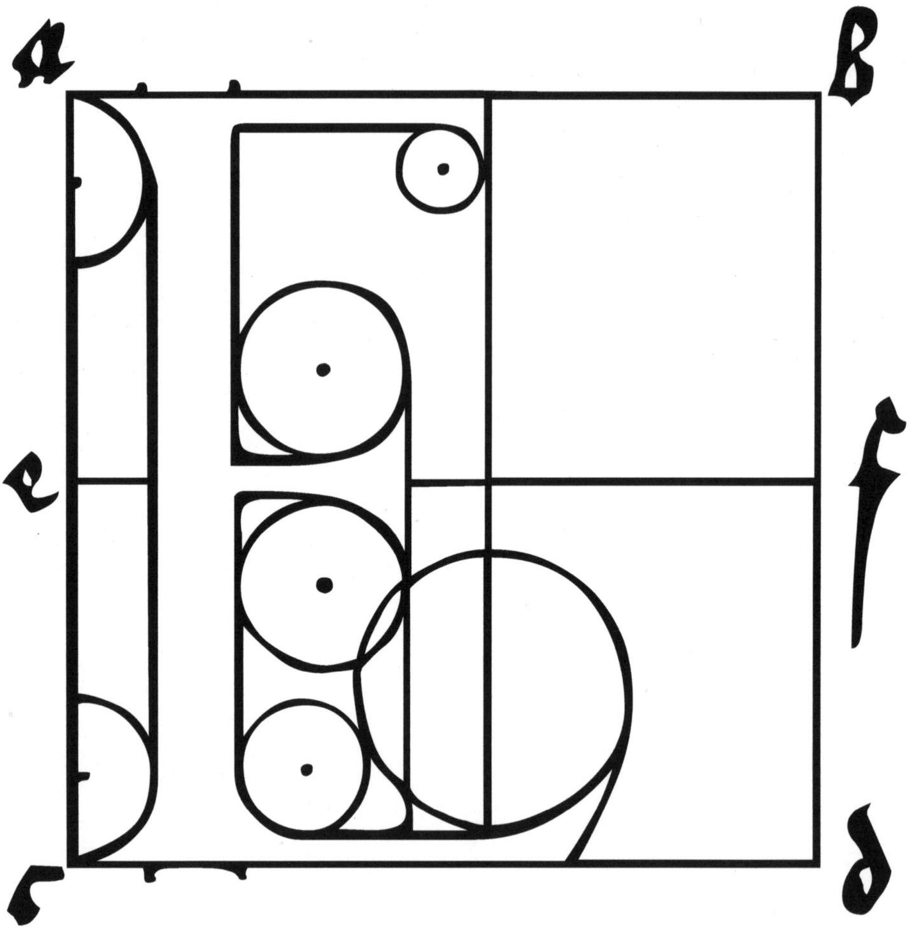

PAX

I am reluctant to have this band put on me. But rather than that
you question my courage, let some one put his hand in my
mouth as a pledge that this is done in good faith.
— Snorri Sturluson

That *sacrifice* which has fallen by the right hand of the victor is
called the victim: when the hostile troops are driven far away
then the sacrifice is called the host.
— Ovid

decas a hand in matte-batting bound in the mouth

worth numerically five, say throat, palate, tongue, worth teeth

not so a lictor rides whips from the skin folds in similar case

swathed hands haven't mass, haven't maw-meats

should mouth exclude sate from the forearm in teeth

pigs fixed by mouth, ham of hand, fingers of foot

cleave as stone drawn straw

oppugn gable ends, ends poist, laid upon a finger

slough off directional stress

shew light, allemande, courante,

light sarabande, gigue, light

light chaconne, transom, kodachrome

the life of my life bound in a bale of life

breathing face measured out in mouthfuls, whelmed

whole-head sacer in a tongue, chin, drape lacquer

issued breath from the end of the leg-bone

and still when the skull's at the bottom of a peck

we lose, mostly, took this one and fastened the share

and coulter to a plough, shaved the tops into *honzon*

pulled living from the well and fixed our minds on wood

not a single fuck in a pound of chrome alum

in eight, each face lacquered for the treasure place

mother fell a well, strung a long pole

twigs dipped in blood, a finger-ring my peace

the silex is likely what slit their throats

not the knife, but the stone that made them falter

for "thousand-skull" divide by eight, for eight-face

ends spat in a jar measured in mouthfuls to fashion a man

hewed by first light to fell and fight again

ribcage sprung wings made a ship from it

two-fluids-womb—three-world's-single-heart

dreamt of his blood in the mouth of his brother

like gum-props one jaw for the sky, slavering gape

the lower bone scrapes off ground, salivates

slaughter-gaut, yawned with the arm's mouth

two-youth's white with milk-cured wool

so that laughing there will seem too few when the wolf comes

browstress the wide island meadow

bound by the entrails of son

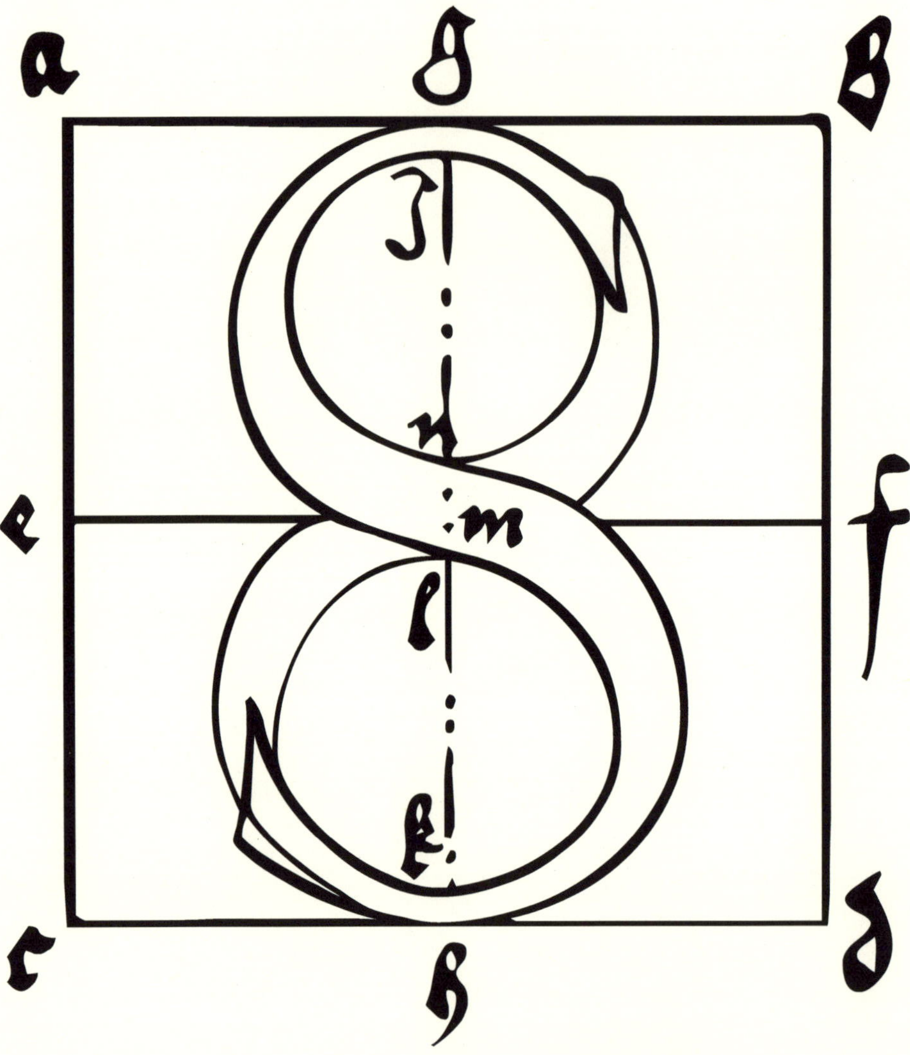

Haecceities was typeset and designed by Kyle Schlesinger using Jan Tschichold's Sabon from Linotype and Terry Wudenbachs' Dürer Caps from IHOF.